Universal Laws: Unlocking the Secrets of the Universe

7 Natural Laws of the Universe

By Creed McGregor

Disclaimer

The information provided in this book is meant to provide helpful information on the subjects discussed. The publisher and author are not responsible for any needs that may require professional supervision and are not liable for any damages or negative consequences from any treatment, action, application or preparation to any person reading or following the information provided in this book. References are provided for informational purposes only and do not constitute endorsement of any websites or other sources.

While attempts have been made to verify that the information contained in this book is accurate, neither the publisher nor author assumes any responsibility for errors, omissions, interpretations, or usage of the subject matters herein.

Table of Contents

Introduction

It's that feeling you get when you look up at the stars or witness a beautiful sunrise. That sense of belonging or being a part of something much larger is deep inside all of us. We all have a higher sense that there is more to life than going to work, paying the bills, and watching television every night.

Is there more out there than this? Who am I really? What is my purpose?

These are questions that many people have started asking themselves. They stem from a sense that we are more than we perceive to be and that there is some other reason or destiny to our existence.

The answers to these questions are hidden in the natural laws of the universe. These irrefutable laws govern ALL things without uncertainty. They shape the world around us as well as our inner being. They do not budge or alter course. The universal laws leave nothing to chance. They do not operate within blurred lines; they only work within specific and well-defined lines. They are not subject to debate.

The only thing left to question is why we're not taught these universal laws in school or anytime during life? Why are they hidden from us and not talked about? Is it because the information is so powerful it could transform our entire existence? Many believe so and agree there are certain authorities that don't want us exploring these laws.

If each person took on the responsibility of learning all they could about the universal laws it would most definitely have a huge impact on life, as we know it, and for the better.

It begins with you! Your outer world is a reflection of your inner world. Personal development within the boundaries of universal laws will elevate you to a higher plane of consciousness. The universal laws are our human spirit guidelines that can help us to achieve great things, to increase our quality of life, and give us hope.

Anything you want to accomplish or manifest in life can be found in the secrets of the universe. They are the key to ALL life and existence!

The Law of Divine Oneness

The Law of One or Oneness – This is the law of original creation. It states that everything is connected. What we think, believe, say, and do will have a corresponding effect on others and the world around us. This is the supreme law over all other laws.

All of humanity and nature are interconnected as one energy source. Some call this source God. We all share in the fact that we are energy. This is what is referred to as our soul or spirit. Everything around us is also energy, living or material. From trees and plants to material things like a desk or chair.

When broken down, everything consists of some type of energy. This may be kinetic, gravitational, chemical, thermal, electrical, magnetic, or mechanical energy. It may be energy that is carried by light or sound. Everything exists as energy. We all interact with one another and all things on some level of energy or consciousness whether we're aware of it or not.

Everything that exists emanates from one source of energy. When one is harmed, we are all harmed. When one is healed, we are all healed. The world does not consist of separate things. Mind and matter are not separate from each other nor are we human beings separate from one another. All humans, nature, elements, minerals, plants, insects, animals and seemingly non-living matter are all connected.

Within the Law of Oneness everything exists. Nothing exists outside this Oneness. This Oneness is endless in terms of time, space, and force. Energy cannot be created or destroyed it only changes form. In relationship to energy nothing dies completely including humans, we only change form. Everything that exists is continually moving or changing form.

Think of a material object like a solid desk. It is continually changing although much too slow for our limited perception to witness. But if you left for 100 years and came back, the desk would be in a different form. It would have deteriorated, which is simply a transformation of its energy caused by the energy and forces around it. This means the desk is continually changing even at this moment. It has changed form and is slightly different, on a molecular level, than it was only a minute ago.

Everything in existence is under this law. Nothing escapes the field of universal energy. This isn't to say we aren't unique as individuals. We are all One but at the same time we are all unique. No one can replace you. Although it is possible to be aware of our individuality we are still at the same time part of the whole. It's hard to say where one ends and another person begins.

Just thinking to ourselves internally distresses the field of energy, which we all exist within. Your thoughts and feelings send out frequencies and vibrations that can be measured. These frequencies attract other like frequencies. Therefore, even our thinking shifts universal energies and creates movement because ALL things are connected. Again, nothing escapes the Law of Oneness.

Being awake to the Law of Divine Oneness can give us a sense of awareness and expand our consciousness. Meditating on this law gives an overwhelming feeling of interconnectedness with ALL.

Knowing that our determinations, desires, and behaviors will begin to align and move things in the direction we desire can have a profound influence on our wishes. When we think, feel, speak, and act in certain ways, things and people are touched either positively or negatively.

This can have an overpowering inspiration on what we think and how we act. Having a sense of Oneness, you begin to become aware of how feeling angry, revengeful, or full of hate can negatively distress the world around you. Being mindful of this may influence you to shift your thinking to a more positive energy.

Being part of a whole and being sensible of Oneness with all nature and human beings should trigger feelings of love. Love is one of the strongest positive emotions. It is the opposite of the negative emotion of fear. It's the highest positive frequency we can produce.

If every human being on earth lived in pure love instead of in fear, life would change, as we know it. Peace and harmony would exist everywhere and nothing in existence would be unaltered for the better.

The Law of Vibration

The Law of Vibration or Frequency – Vibrational energy is the essence of this law. It is the foundation of the better known Law of Attraction. In the previous chapter on the Law of Divine Oneness we touched upon vibration and frequency. We also learned that everything is energy.

When we look on a subatomic level at any substance we do not find matter, but rather pure energy. Energy that is constantly vibrating and moving. Nothing rests, including human beings. However, your frequencies and vibrations are different from other beings and things in the universe.

This does not mean we are separate, it means we are all unique in our own vibrational patterns like fingerprints, but we all exist in one ocean of vibrating energy. Everything has its own unique vibrational frequency like a table, a desk, a chair, a rock, and even our thoughts and feelings. The Law of Vibration governs it all.

Let's use a desk as an example again. It may appear to be solid and still but remember it's always moving, vibrating, and constantly changing form. Science has proven this with the invention of the microscope. We can see millions of subatomic particles vibrating and moving with energy meaning the desk is pure energy and emits its own unique vibrations.

So what seems like a separate solid desk sitting on its own is actually an illusion. It is the Law of Vibration in action. However we don't perceive it as vibrational energy until we break it down to subatomic particles and view it with a microscope. This proves that vibrational frequencies exist even if we can't see them with the naked eye.

We have to remain open minded that there are things around us that exist outside of our 5 senses. Meaning that just because we can't verify it with our immediate senses doesn't mean it isn't real. A dog whistle for example isn't a frequency human's limited hearing can detect, yet we know it exists because it's been proven that dogs can hear it.

Many things were thought fact or impossible to exist until science proved it wrong. The world was once flat until proven differently. We were told our galaxy, the Milky Way was the only galaxy, but now we know there are billions of other galaxies. If you were to tell someone 100 years ago we could communicate wirelessly they would have locked you up for being crazy.

In the near future everyone will accept that everything is energy and that everything vibrates and radiates frequency. The Law of

Vibration will be taught in school just like the Law of Gravity. This will be our greatest advancement in understanding the world around us.

Many inventors throughout history have been accused of being crazy or nuts because it was outside the frame of knowledge at that time. People did not have the capacity to grasp inventions or theories like radio waves, electricity, magnetic fields, and even the Internet.

The fact is, whether you believe it or not, we live in an ocean of motion. Our thoughts and emotions, no matter what they are, at every second of our lives are sending out vibrational frequencies. We have the power to change our frequencies so we can tune into anything we want in life. You will begin to understand the true benefit of this law as it ties into the next chapter.

The Law of Attraction

Also known as The Law of Manifestation – This law is probably the most well known and talked about law. All of the universal laws are tied together but this law is very closely related to the Law of Vibration. The Law of Vibration is the foundation of The Law of Attraction.

The Law of Vibration says everything emits a vibrational frequency including our thoughts and feelings. The Law of Attraction takes it a step further and states "like attracts like." In other words, vibrational energies attract other like vibrational energies whether positive or negative.

Whether we realize it or not, we are responsible for attracting both positive and negative circumstances into our lives. Whatever we place our focus and energy on will have a direct impact on what happens to us. Like many teachers in the past have stated, "You become what you think about." In the Bible it's Galatians 6:7 that reads, "For whatever one sows, that will he also reap."

When we know that our thoughts and feelings are vibrating (Law of Vibration) and that like attracts like (Law of Attraction) we begin to fathom how we can alter our lives just by altering our thoughts and emotions. This is however a two edged sword because you can attract negative energies into your life just as easily, if not easier than positive energies.

The problem lies within our subconscious mind where many beliefs have been encoded from childhood. Many suffer today as adults because of things they were told and programmed to believe as children. Thoughts and emotions of worry, fear, scarcity, sickness, death, and so on have afflicted us all.

When you have negative thoughts or beliefs in your life about relationships, money, or the future, you'll likely see more negativity in those areas because like energies attract like energies. The blessing is we can learn to reprogram our thoughts and belief system to begin attracting positive energies into our lives. This is the Law of Attraction at its core.

By purposefully manipulating or changing our thought process we can begin to attract the things into our lives that we desire. It is however easier said than done. Experts say we have to do more than just wish for things. You can't just cut out a picture of a sports car, if that's what you desire, look at it everyday and hope it will someday appear.

You have to really want something and give intense attention and focus to it. You also have to go deeper into your soul and change your belief system that's been programmed into your subconscious mind. For example, you may say you want a new sports car and talk about it all the time, but if deep down you do not truly believe it will happen or if you have the belief that you really don't deserve it, it will never happen!

The Law of Attraction only brings to you the same like energies that you are emitting from your true feelings and emotions, not just from physical thinking. You have to feel and believe it can happen. Your feelings and emotions have to be aligned and in harmony with your desires.

When you're angry, upset, depressed, or full of hate you notice that bad things keep happening to you, right? People keep hurting you, things don't go your way, the world is out to get you, and so on. You are getting back the like negative energies that you are putting out.

The same goes for positive energies, only you have to "fall in love" with what you want in order to tune into the right vibrational state. As mentioned earlier love is the strongest positive energy we can send out so using it to tune into the frequencies of your desires will prove favorable.

The Law of Attraction dictates everything in your life good or bad. Nothing happens by coincidence or by accident. If you are constantly worried you're going to get in a car wreck then you will most likely get in a car wreck. If you fear more than anything being robbed then you will most likely someday get robbed. Nothing happens by chance. We attract whatever we're focused on most and give the most feeling to.

This phenomenon can happen on a much larger scale as well. One might think that cancer rates are declining with the increase in testing, research, and awareness for prevention and a cure. Unfortunately they aren't. Cancer rates have actually increased steadily over the years. Why? Because all of the attention and awareness we are giving to cancer is actually causing more cancer. We should be focusing on being fit, healthy, chemical and pollution free and not focused on the disease itself.

The thing to remember when it comes to The Law of Attraction is that it's going to happen whether we're aware of it or not. It's happened your entire life. You've attracted every situation or circumstance you've ever been in. You attract every person, place, or event that injects your life whether you purposefully mean to or not.

Obviously people, things, and events are not attracted to you instantly, they take time to develop. But nonetheless they will develop. If you're on the right frequency but suddenly change your mind or your beliefs about something before it has reached you, it will begin to drift away. If your energies change because of doubt or fear then you'll begin to attract the new like energies.

To manifest desires and bring closer your most treasured ambitions, you have to channel your focus on the energies you want to attract for as long as it takes to attract them. Unfortunately, giving up hope or quitting short of the goal line happens all too often. When people don't see results or get instant gratification, doubt creeps in and they begin shifting their focus. So remember to stay focused and be patient!

Creative Visualization – To keep those positive frequencies in tune with your desires you can learn to use some techniques. One of these techniques is creative visualization. In almost a meditative state that some refer to as daydreaming, we can focus our energies and feelings on a particular need or desire. Painting a picture in your mind of having your desire or achieving a goal can create intense feelings and emotions.

Creative visualization is a great way to "fall in love" with your ambitions. Picturing yourself already achieving what it is you want to achieve will radiate intense vibrational frequencies that will help attract like energies. This will help an ambition manifest much faster. Sending out these frequencies will begin to shift the universal energies necessary to move the people, things, and events towards you that will be necessary to see an ambition through.

Athletes use creative visualization all the time to achieve goals. They will envision themselves winning a race, accomplishing new feats, or breaking a record to help manifest them into reality.

It's important to note that when you desire something and begin to tune your dial into its energies, you must not concern yourself with "how" it's going to happen. That isn't your concern. Let the universal energies around you work that out, do not try to interfere. In other words, stay out of your own way.

For example, if it's more money you desire for doing good with, all you have to do is focus your energy on that ambition. See yourself having more money. Do not try to come up with your own ways of making more money. Just trust in the Law of Attraction and the way will be shown to you. The universe will let you know when you need to take action. We will learn more about this in the chapter on The Law of Action.

Using positive affirmations – Another technique used in the Law of Attraction is affirmations in the form of internal thoughts or spoken words. You can use affirmations to reflect your vision of the things you desire. Many people speak affirmations into the mirror each morning.

This technique helps shape, or reshape, your core beliefs and ambitions. Repeating affirming words daily will promote consistent optimism into your focused energy, which will help radiate the right vibrations through your true feelings and emotions.

Keep a list of positive affirmations handy and read them often. It is also best to use them in a present tense. For example, if you desire more money but find that you have a false belief from childhood that money is evil, then you should repeat affirmations like the following:

Money is good and I use it only for good things

I use money to help those in need and make the world a better place

Money is my tool to get the things I need to succeed in life

Money makes me a better person and is not used in a negative way

I am grateful for being wealthy and having all the abundance I desire

Keeping your affirmations in present tense and focusing on the positive aspects of it will help send out the right vibrational frequency. Affirmations will also remind you of your course and help you stay positive and on track throughout the day.

I have written several books that each have 500 affirmations on topics like money, wealth, abundance, success, and happiness. You can find them under my name in the Amazon bookstore.

The Law of Action

The Law of Action – This law states that we must take action to get what we desire. In the previous chapter we talked about the Law of Attraction and focusing on your most treasured ambitions. It was also mentioned not to worry about "how" it would happen but to trust the universe to show you the way. This is where the Law of Action comes into play.

There is a fine line between YOU trying to figure out how to accomplish a goal and the universe showing you how. It's important to know the difference. In most cases, if you're paying attention, you'll know when you're supposed to take action. The problem is as soon as most people focus on a new desire they instantly try to think of ways to make it happen. This is interfering with the cosmos. They are essentially getting in their own way.

Focus on the desire, meditate on it, visualize having achieved it, and then listen for the universe to give you direction. No you aren't going to be hit by a bolt of lightening followed by a God like voice directing your next move, although you might, but have faith that you will know when you're being pointed in a certain direction. You will know what to do as long as you are listening.

Once we've been given direction then we have to act. We must engage in actions that support our desires. Taking action in harmony with our thoughts and dreams in an orderly fashion towards want it is we want to accomplish is the premise of the Law of Action. The enemies of this law are fear and laziness, which we will talk about shortly.

Some actions will be easier than others depending on your desire. If it were your desire to go somewhere special on vacation you would first have that thought and then visualize upon it. Perhaps you might make a goal chart for financing the vacation. Then start looking up prices, flights, hotels, and other activities to do in the area. These actions will begin to move the necessary energies closer to you achieving your vacation. Simply sitting there each day and visualizing about the vacation may not result in much. Action is the key.

You should be able to start understanding the chain effect each law as on one another and how they all work in unison. You first have a positive thought and send out the right vibrations, which start to attract the things you want in life, and then you are shown what actions to take to eventually manifest your desires. So thought equals vibration equals attraction of like energies equals what action to take equals manifested desires.

Still on the subject of the Law of Action, some may be asking, "How do I know if I'm taking the right action?" This is a very good question. When you suspect you're being shown which direction to move don't hesitate. You won't always know if you're on the right path but if you move in a general direction of your desires, doors will start to open for you. No matter how small the action, it can have a huge impact as other opportunities begin to emerge.

Like a chain reaction of dominos, things will just start falling into place. Most of all just have faith in the universe and the cosmic laws. You may get off course or stumble along the way but as long as you keep moving forward continuing to take action you will eventually manifest your desires.

Be wary of fear and laziness. These negative action-busting emotions will stop your desires from coming true. You have to recognize these emotions in order to conquer them. Do not let them get in the way of the Law of Action, push through them with every fiber of your being.

The Law of Action is not easy, but we know it tells us unless we take action nothing will happen. Visualization and affirmations are excellent techniques and they're necessary but will only get you so far. Action is the key.

I can't help but think of someone going to a conference to hear an excellent motivational speaker. They listen, take notes all weekend, and leave there gleaming with excitement and full of new ideas only to get back home and have fear or laziness keep them from taking action.

Perhaps you've been there yourself. Those new ideas and creative juices are the direction they've been shown but then they fail to follow the Law of Action. After a few days the excitement defuses and nothing changes. This is sad but it happens all the time. So remember, action is the key!

The Law of Correspondence

Also known as the Law of Equivalence – This universal law states that the principles of physics that explain the physical world of energy, light, vibration, and motion have their corresponding principles in the universe. "As above, so below," "As within, so without" or "Whatever is above is like that which is below, and whatever is below is like that which is above."

Confused yet? Basically this law is the old adage you may have heard, that our outer world is a reflection of our inner world. It is probably one of the most important universal laws that exist if we had to choose one. It is the foundation of almost all self-help courses that teach us to change from the inside out.

If your life is filled with unhappiness, depression, chaos, or just lacking satisfaction, it's because it's reflecting what's inside you. If we clench negative thoughts and beliefs internally, then our outer world becomes one of turmoil and discord.

The Law of Correspondence shows us the dangers of grasping onto negative thoughts. It proves that any negative circumstances or situation in our lives are essentially self-inflicting. Most people do not like to hear that but it's true according to the law.

When we start to feel bad inside we perceive our outer world as bad, meaning we only see bad around us. The worse the outer world becomes, the worse we feel inside and it becomes a vicious cycle that can be hard to break.

There is a direct correspondence between the way you think and feel internally and the way you experience your outer world. So in order to change our outer world, circumstances, and situations, we must first take a look in the mirror and begin to change inside. No matter how hard we try, we cannot change our outer world if we don't change our inner world first.

This law, like the other laws is irrefutable. Your reality will ALWAYS be a reflection of your inner thoughts, feelings, and beliefs. The Law of Correspondence says the only way to get what we truly want in life is to change our thoughts.

This can be a difficult task for some. It is much easier to blame others or to blame circumstances for our misfortunes. It is also much kinder on our egos to blame someone else than to take responsibility. But until we accept this law nothing will change. It is you, it is your fault, and you are responsible for whatever turmoil, chaos, or unhappiness you have in your life right now. Accept that and you can begin to change your life for the better.

To escape turmoil, stop trying to change the world around you from the outside. To change your outer world you have to make a paradigm shift. You have to change your patterns of negative feelings and beliefs because they have a direct impact on your attitude and ultimately your outer world. Take a long hard look at yourself. Try to pinpoint the reasons you have inner turmoil, negative beliefs, and so on. Take responsibility and stop blaming others.

For a long time I blamed my own Mother for most of my unfavorable situations in life, even in adulthood. I blamed her for my alcoholism, my dismal financial situation, my unhappy marriage, and so on. It wasn't until I took responsibility by looking in the mirror that my inner world began to change and eventually my outer world started to follow. Now I've been sober for 15 years, I'm well on my way to being wealthy, and my marriage is stronger than ever. None of this is by chance. It is the Law of Correspondence in action.

If you want positive change in your life, look internally. Look in the mirror and the person you are inside. By changing the quality of your thoughts, you will change the quality of your life. It isn't a mystery; it's an indisputable law that most people aren't even aware of.

The fact that you are reading this book is a sign that you're willing to accept responsibility for where you are in life. Most likely you're ready for change and now you know it begins internally. Begin today to work on yourself and your entire outer world will begin to follow.

The Law of Cause and Effect

Also known as Karma – This law states that nothing happens by chance and that all actions have consequences and produce specific results. The choices we make and actions we take, or don't take, whether conscious or unconscious, have corresponding outcomes and effects.

This law, like the other laws, works without question whether you're aware of it or not. A specific trigger causes every outcome in your life. Excess and uncontrollable spending causes money problems or debt. Speeding and having a lead foot results in getting a speeding ticket. A poor diet and lack of exercise result in poor health.

The Law of Cause and Effect is the universal version of the physical law Sir Isaac Newton gave us, the Law of Motion, which states for every action there is an equal and opposite reaction. There is always a corresponding cause or effect assigned to the nature of our actions.

Looking at this law from more of a quantum physics point of view we can see it's responsible for how the universe has progressed. Every cause has an effect and every effect becomes the cause of something else. So it implies that the universe is always in motion, which we also learned in the Law of Divine Oneness, and that it has progressed to where it is today from a chain of events. One effect causing another effect causing another and so on.

This law is also the foundation of the Butterfly Effect in the chaos theory. It's basis is cause and effect and states that a small change (butterfly wings flapping) one on side of the world can result in a large change several weeks later in a weather pattern such as a tornado.

It simply suggests that a butterfly's wings might create tiny changes in the atmosphere that may ultimately alter the path of a tornado or delay, accelerate, or even prevent the occurrence of a tornado in another location. The butterfly does not directly create the tornado; it only disturbs its pattern according to the theory.

If nothing else this shows us how the Law of Cause and Effect forms our entire universe and the world around us. Although we cannot predict every effect a cause may have like in the tornado example, we can still apply it to our own lives.

This law in the spiritual realm is called Karma. If we exhibit a positive force in words or actions, a positive energy will come back to us. This is also true with negative forces. You cannot do something dishonest or wrong without something bad coming back to you.
Even if you're the only one who knows you did something wrong you cannot escape it. Those

forces will come back around and negatively impact your outer world.

This law helps those that are aware of it to stay on a straight path. Being honest, thankful, giving, and unselfish will reap you great rewards in your life. Once mankind trusts and believes in this law it will have a positive effect on the entire universe.

The Law of Rhythm

This could also be called the Law of Flow – This universal law tells us that everything flows in the universe. Everything has rhythm, all things flow in and out, and all things rise and fall. The pendulum swings back and forth in everything. If something swings to the right, it must then swing to the left.

The Law of Rhythm can be seen in the waves and tides of the ocean. Everything in existence is involved in a beautiful dance swaying, flowing, and swinging back and forth, up and down. Everything is either growing or dying.

This law can even be seen in the rise and fall of empires, in the business cycles of great companies, economic cycles, in your thoughts from positive to negative, and then back to positive again like a pendulum.

The basis of this law says that a thing begins to slow as it reaches a peaking point before beginning a backward swing in the opposite direction. It then peaks on the other end and then repeats the whole process. It is this law that determines seasons, cycles, stages, and patterns in ALL things.

The Law of Rhythm governs our health, relationships, spirituality, and economy. What seems random is actually very orderly and in perfect rhythm. Once you reach a peak in your fitness you may begin to plateau and then start to swing backwards. If you own a business you may see your profits fluctuate up and down over the years.

Rising above this law – In order to rise above the Law of Rhythm and avoid a downswing in any part of your life you have to become aware of the backward swing of the pendulum. The key to success in mastering this law is balance. By never allowing your emotions or feelings to swing too far in one direction you can create more balance.

Do not become discouraged when you feel the drawback of any endeavor in your life be it health, relationships, finances, or your career. Fight through to remain positive no matter how far back the law pulls you. Know that this too shall pass, and that things will eventually swing back in your favor again.

This is where perseverance and consistence are good hands to play. Each swing backward will become less powerful as you understand how the law works. Staying positive and swinging further in the right direction each time will elevate you to great heights.

Conclusion

Knowing and understanding how these 7 universal laws work will give you great insight into your true existence. As we humans begin applying and working with these laws instead of fighting again them, our planet will begin to change for the better.

Mankind in fact, is on an upward swing of the pendulum according to astrologists. We are swinging out of the Dark Ages when the Sun and the star Sirius were at their greatest distance from one another. They've orbited through the bottom curve and are now drawing closer once again. At their closest we human beings are in a frequency of complete love and awake to pure consciousness. This is the Law of Rhythm at work.

In the near future we will become more aware of our energy being. We will start to awaken to pure consciousness and tune into more of a love frequency as opposed to fear. We will begin to connect to other conscious beings and comprehend more about parallel universe theories that quantum physics tells us about.

We'll become more intelligent as we learn to open up and use parts or our minds that have been dormant. We've already noticed great technological advances in recent years but it's just the tip of the iceberg.

Scientists tell us that only 8% of our DNA is functional. We'll begin to use new channels in the other 92% of our own DNA, which will give us biological advancements that are impossible for us to currently comprehend.

These universal laws are the basis of all existence. Everyone will come into their own awareness when they are ready. Some may choose to stay in the dark ages. We're seeing the remnants of that in the crime, war, killing, and hatred that still exists.

Why don't we hear more about these universal laws and how they govern ALL things?

This may come as a shock to you, but there are those out there that don't want us to advance as a species, not as a whole anyway. They are blinded by power and greed.

People in very powerful positions control our entire population like a bunch of sheep. We are referred to as "sheeple." Our complete political and economic system is a well-oiled machine that serves only a handful of people. We are in the midst of economic slavery and the most evil type of slavery is enslaving those that aren't even aware they're slaves.

These powers control mass media to determine what we see and don't see. They keep us in the dark and in fear far away from love. They keep us entertained, fat, and distracted. Under the disguise of powerful corporations our entire planet is held in limbo because of selfish agendas.

This is not conspiracy theory when we say these powers control everything! Their military-industrial complex controls the food we eat, the pills we take, the state of the economy, our monetary system, medical system, TV shows, movies, and newspapers we read, to the oil, gas, and coal we depend on.

Events are manipulated so to benefit an egotistical plan. Things are hidden from us that might give us hope. We even attack our own country to create fear and to have an excuse to go to war to achieve a predetermined mission. This demonstration of power and control goes against the natural laws of the universe.

It's a fact that right now we have the technology to move beyond gas-powered transportation. We have magnetic energy technology that can manipulate gravity to create propulsion based UFO type space vehicles.

Unfortunately these technologies are buried as quickly as they surface. People have been threatened, harmed, and even worse in order to keep these technologies hidden. Why? Because these powers control our current economy and it keeps them very rich and very powerful.

It's up to us as spiritual energy beings to not fight against them, but to connect to the universe on a higher plane so we can evolve towards a love frequency and a pure conscious state.

They cannot stop the pendulum from swinging. Political change will come, Governments will fall, and we will stop being dependent on things that harm our planet and keep us from being who we truly are.

Deep down you know there is more out there than what you perceive. When you look up at the stars at night or witness a beautiful sunrise it confirms there is more to life than what we're told. We aren't meant to be economic slaves, or to kill each other, or to destroy our own planet. Universal law will prevail. You can choose to fight against it or to be open to it.

Soak up information and learn all you can about cosmic laws, quantum physics, spirituality, mysticism, and so on. Connect with the universe through meditation, prayer, channeling, affirmations, and controlled thought. Find the frequency of love internally and resist all negativity.

Feel the Divine Oneness of ALL things and know you are part of something much larger than your current reality may be showing you. Be part of the movement that expands our minds and opens are spirits to a new existence. Connect with the universe and listen for the answers to guide you. There is more to our existence and it can be found in the universal laws as well as inside each and every one of us.

If you enjoyed this book and would like to help spread this vital information I'd like to ask you for a favor. Would you be kind enough to leave a review for this book on Amazon? I would greatly appreciate it. Thank you!

Printed in Great Britain
by Amazon